W9-BWF-461

DATE DUE

A cat dressed in Christmas ribbons

Christmas

Steve Potts

A⁺

Smart Apple Media

Published by Smart Apple Media

1980 Lookout Drive, North Mankato, MN 56003

Designed by Rita Marshall

Printed in the United States of America

Photographs by Archive Photos, Curtis Martin, Louisa Preston, Mrs. Kevin Scheibel, The Viesti Collection (Bavaria, Cummins)

Library of Congress Cataloging-in-Publication Data

Potts, Steve. Christmas / by Steve Potts. p. cm. – (Holidays series)

Includes bibliographical references and index.

ISBN 1-58340-115-6

1. Christmas–Juvenile literature. [1. Christmas. 2. Holidays.] I. Title.

GT4985.5 .P68 2001   394.2663–dc21   00-067906

First Edition 9 8 7 6 5 4 3 2 1

Christmas

CONTENTS

Holiday Greetings

December 25, Christmas, is a special day for people of the Christian faith. During this holiday, many families around the world gather to celebrate the birth of Jesus Christ. They may exchange presents, make special foods, attend church, and sing carols. **Nativity** scenes, decorated trees, cards, and **Santa Claus** may all be part of the Christmas holiday. No one knows exactly when Jesus was born, but around 300 A.D., the Roman Catholic Church made December

A stained glass scene of the birth of Christ

25 a holiday. One of the reasons they chose this day to cele-

brate Christ's birthday was because it was near the winter sol-

stice. It was also the date of an ancient pagan festival held in

honor of a sun god. By choosing December **People who collect old Christmas postcards may**

25, the Catholics hoped to inspire the pagans

to worship the "son of God" instead of the **pay hundreds of dollars for certain ones.**

"sun." As the years passed, Christmas

became one of the holiest days on the Christian calendar.

Even though the reason for celebrating Christmas is the same

around the world, Christmas traditions may vary. One custom

is for people to send each other Christmas cards. Today, most

people send cards purchased in a store. But that was not

always true. Originally, people sent each other homemade

A printed Christmas card from the late 1800s

Trees lit with strings of Christmas lights

cards. In the 1840s, English businesses began designing and printing cards. These cards were soon sold and sent around the world. Today, millions of Christmas cards are mailed each year to family members and friends.

Christmas Kisses

Another Christmas custom is the use of **mistletoe**. More than 2,000 years ago, the Druids, the priests in the British Isles, burned mistletoe as a way to worship their gods and celebrate the start of winter. They also put small pieces of mistletoe in their homes as symbols of joy. The ancient

A Christmas Greeting

The acorn suggests that I welcome my friend
'Neath the holly and mistletoe bough;
So a greeting I send ere Christmas shall end,
And I hope you will come to me now

Scandinavians also valued mistletoe. In their customs, mistletoe belonged to the goddess of love. They honored this goddess by kissing when they saw mistletoe. A holiday tradition

Holly berries and mistletoe

still practiced today says that when people catch you under the mistletoe, they get to kiss you.

Decorated Trees

One of the most beautiful holiday traditions is the Christmas tree. In the 1500s, Germans began decorating fir trees with paper ornaments, apples, and candy to celebrate Christmas. Candles may have been put on a Christmas tree for the first time by **Martin Luther**. By the 1800s, the Christmas tree tradition had spread to England. Queen Victoria's husband, Albert, was a German. When Albert

married Victoria, he asked her if she would put up a Christmas

tree. She agreed, and the tradition of the Christmas tree

gradually came to England. 🌰 Christmas trees came to North

America in the early 1800s with the **Pennsylvania Dutch**.

More than 100 years later, after the discovery of electricity,

electric light bulbs replaced Christmas tree

candles. Wrapped presents and small models

of the Nativity are often found beneath

Christmas trees. The Nativity scene, or crèche,

The custom of burning a yule log symbolizes giving up bad feelings.

may be made of wood, plastic, or plaster. Some churches even

have "live" Nativity scenes, complete with real sheep, donkeys,

and camels.

A drawing of the original St. Nicholas

A Jolly Old Man

Santa Claus, perhaps the oldest Christmas tradition, is based on a real person. The original St. Nicholas was born in the fourth century in Turkey. Nicholas, who became a priest, was known for his kindness and love for children. Nicholas died on December 6, 342. That day became St. Nicholas's feast day. By the 1500s, the tradition of St. Nicholas had spread to Europe. In England he was known as Father Christmas. The Dutch called him *Sint Nikolass*. When the Dutch settled in New York in the early 1600s, they brought their Christmas

traditions with them. Sint Nikolass became *Sinterklass*, or, as

he's called today, Santa Claus. The image of the modern

Santa Claus came from a poem written in 1822, "The Night

Santa Claus and his sack of presents

Before Christmas." This poem described a jolly old man who came down chimneys. He also filled stockings with toys and drove a sleigh pulled by flying reindeer. In 1870, cartoonist Thomas Nast first drew the fat man in a red suit that most people today recognize as Santa. Christmas celebrations may include many customs from many different cultures.

Filled with beautiful sights and sounds, Christmas is a season of joy and giving.

The poinsettia is a traditional Christmas plant that originally grew on tropical islands.

Red poinsettia plants

Christmas Activity

The gingerbread house is an old Christmas tradition that you can add to your family's holiday fun.

What You Need

8–10 graham crackers
An empty one-pint (47 ml) carton (opened like a box)
A tray
Colorful hard candies (gumdrops, sprinkles, etc.)
Tube frosting with varied tips (any bright color)
White frosting

What You Do

Cover the carton with white frosting and set it on the tray. Attach four graham crackers to the carton's sides for walls. Lay one graham cracker on top of the carton. This will be the base of the roof. "Glue" it on with frosting. Lean two graham crackers on the roof's base and "glue" them with frosting. Decorate the house with white frosting "snow." Use tube frosting to make windows and a door. Finally, add the candies.

A house decorated for Christmas

INFORMATION

Index

Words to Know

Martin Luther–founder of the Lutheran church

mistletoe–a yellow and green plant with white berries

Nativity–the birth of Jesus Christ

Pennsylvania Dutch–a group of German immigrants who settled in Pennsylvania in the 1700s

Santa Claus–the North American name for St. Nicholas and Sinterklass

Read More

Christmas Around the World: A Celebration. New York: Sterling Publishing Company, 1978.

Fischer, Sara, and Barbara Klebanow. *American Holidays: Exploring Traditions, Customs, and Backgrounds.* Brattleboro, Vt.: Pro Lingua Associates, 1986.

Kalman, Bobbie. *Christmas Long Ago from A to Z.* New York: Crabtree Publishing Company, 1999.

Kindersley, Anabel. *Celebrations.* New York: DK Publishing, 1997.

Internet Sites

Christmas 'Round the World
http://www.auburn.edu/~vestmon/christmas.html

Christmas.com
http://www.Christmas.com

Christmas! Christmas! Christmas!
http://www.night.net/Christmas

The Christmas Pages
http://www.north-pole.co.uk/